Oman Travel Guide

Geography and Climate of Oman,
Omani History and Culture,
Accommodation tips, Clothing tips,
Food and Drinks, Tourist Attractions
Car Rental Services /Tour Guide
Companies and Safety Tips

Richard D. Bryden

Copyright

Table of content

Introduction

Oman is a country located in the southeastern coast of the Arabian Peninsula in Western Asia. It shares borders with the United Arab Emirates to the northwest, Saudi Arabia to the west, and Yemen to the southwest. The country has a diverse landscape that includes deserts, mountains, and coastlines along the Arabian Sea, Gulf of Oman, and the Strait of Hormuz.

Oman has a rich cultural history that dates back thousands of years, with evidence of human habitation dating back to the Stone Age. It has been ruled by various dynasties over the centuries, and gained independence from Portugal in 1650. The current Sultan of Oman is Haitham bin Tariq Al Said, who succeeded Qaboos bin Said Al Said in 2020.

Oman is known for its natural beauty, traditional architecture, and vibrant culture. The country is a popular tourist destination, attracting visitors with its historic forts, beautiful beaches, and rich cultural heritage. The economy of Oman is primarily based on oil and gas exports, although efforts have been made in recent years to diversify the economy and promote non-oil sectors such as tourism, manufacturing, and agriculture.

Here are some common daily activities in Oman that you may find throughout the week:

Monday:

People typically start their week with work or school.

Some businesses and government offices may have shorter hours on Mondays.

In the evening, locals may gather with friends or family for dinner or other social events.

Tuesday:

Similar to Monday, most people will be at work or school during the day.

In the evening, some families may participate in cultural activities or events, such as attending a traditional dance or music performance.

Wednesday:

Work or school continues as usual during the day.

Wednesday evenings are often reserved for sports, such as football (soccer), cricket, or tennis.

Thursday:

Thursday is considered the start of the weekend in Oman, and many businesses and government offices have shorter hours or are closed.

Some families may visit the mosque for prayer or attend a religious study group.

Many people may also go shopping or run errands during the day.

In the evening, locals may gather for a barbecue or other outdoor activities.

Friday:

Friday is the official weekend day in Oman, and most businesses and government offices are closed.

Many families attend the mosque for prayer or listen to a religious sermon.

In the afternoon, locals may gather with friends or family for a traditional Omani meal or visit one of the many cultural attractions, such as a museum or fort.

Saturday:

Saturday is also a weekend day in Oman, and many people take the opportunity to relax and spend time with family and friends.

Some families may take a day trip to one of Oman's many natural attractions, such as the mountains or the beach.

In the evening, locals may attend a concert or other entertainment event.
Sunday:

Sunday is the start of the work and school week, and most people will be back to their usual routines.

In the evening, families may gather for dinner or participate in other leisure activities.

I: Geography and Climate of Oman

Oman is a country located on the southeastern coast of the Arabian Peninsula in Western Asia. It is bordered by the United Arab Emirates to the northwest, Saudi Arabia to the west, and Yemen to the southwest. Oman also has a coastline along the Arabian Sea to the south and the Gulf of Oman to the northeast. Oman's geography is characterized by a mix of mountains, desert, and coastline.

The northern part of Oman is dominated by the Al Hajar Mountains, which run parallel to the coast and rise to an elevation of over 3,000 meters. This rugged mountain range is home to Oman's highest peak, Jebel Shams, which stands at 3,009 meters. The Al Hajar Mountains are also known for their stunning wadis (dry riverbeds), which provide a dramatic contrast to the arid landscape. The mountainous terrain gives way to the Al Batinah coastal plain, a narrow strip of land that stretches along the Gulf of Oman and is home to most of Oman's population.

To the south of the Al Hajar Mountains lies the Al Dhahirah region, which is characterized by rolling hills and valleys. The desert occupies much of the central and southern parts of Oman, including the Rub' al Khali (Empty Quarter), one of the largest sand deserts in the world. Despite its harsh conditions, the desert is home to a number of plant and animal species, including the Arabian oryx, which was once extinct in the wild but has been reintroduced in Oman's desert regions.

Oman's climate is largely arid and hot, with temperatures frequently exceeding 40 degrees Celsius in the summer months. The country experiences two distinct seasons: a hot and dry summer from May to October, and a cooler and wetter winter from November to April. The coastal regions experience relatively high humidity, particularly in the summer months, while the interior and desert regions are much drier. The country is also prone to occasional tropical cyclones, which can bring heavy rainfall and strong winds to the coastal areas.

Oman's diverse geography and climate have shaped its history and culture. The mountainous terrain has provided a natural barrier against invaders, while the desert has been home to nomadic Bedouin tribes for centuries. The country's coastline has also played a significant role in its history, with Oman being a major center of trade and commerce for centuries. Today, Oman's natural beauty and unique cultural heritage continue to attract visitors from around the world.

II:Omani History and Culture

Oman is a country located in the Middle East, bordered by the United Arab Emirates, Saudi Arabia, and Yemen. Its rich history and unique culture have been shaped by its strategic location on the Arabian Peninsula and its long history of trade and commerce.

History:

The history of Oman dates back thousands of years, with evidence of human settlement in the region dating back to the Stone Age. The ancient civilization of Magan, which flourished between 3500 and 2000 BC, was based in what is now Oman and was known for its advanced metallurgy and trading links with Mesopotamia.

Over the centuries, Oman was ruled by a succession of powerful empires, including the Persians, the Parthians, the Seleucids, and the Sasanians. In the 7th century, Oman converted to Islam and became part of the Arab Caliphate. During the medieval period, Oman became a major center of trade and commerce, with its sailors and merchants traveling throughout the Indian Ocean and beyond.

In the 16th century, Oman became a major maritime power under the rule of the powerful Al-Busaidi dynasty, which expanded its influence throughout the Persian Gulf, East Africa, and the Indian Ocean. In the 19th century, Oman became a British protectorate, which helped to modernize the country's infrastructure and institutions.

Culture:

Oman has a rich and diverse cultural heritage, which reflects its long history of trade and commerce and its location at the crossroads of several civilizations. The country's culture is characterized by its unique blend of Arab, African, and Indian influences, which have shaped its art, music, cuisine, and traditional dress.

One of the most distinctive aspects of Omani culture is its traditional dress, which includes the dishdasha, a long, flowing robe, and the kumma, a round, embroidered cap. Women typically wear a colorful headscarf, called the hijab, and a long, flowing dress.

Omani cuisine is also unique and reflects the country's diverse cultural heritage. The traditional Omani meal typically includes rice, meat, and vegetables, along with a variety of spices and herbs. Some of the most popular Omani dishes include shuwa, a slow-roasted lamb or goat, and harees, a hearty wheat porridge.

Omani music is also an important aspect of the country's cultural heritage, with traditional instruments such as the oud, the rebaba, and the doumbek being popular among musicians. Traditional dances such as the Razha, which involves the swirling of swords, and the Liwa, a celebratory dance, are also an important part of Omani culture.

In recent years, Oman has also become a popular tourist destination, with visitors from around the world coming to experience its rich history and culture. The country's stunning natural beauty, including its rugged mountains, pristine beaches, and sparkling deserts, also draws visitors from far and wide.

Bedouin Culture in Oman.

Oman is a country with a diverse cultural heritage, and one unique culture in Oman is the Bedouin culture. Bedouins are traditionally nomadic people who move from place to place in search of grazing land for their herds of camels, sheep, and goats. Bedouin culture is deeply rooted in the country's history and has played a significant role in shaping Omani culture.

The Bedouin people of Oman have a distinct lifestyle, customs, and traditions. They live in tents made of goat hair or wool and move from place to place depending on the season and availability of water and grazing land. Their diet consists mainly of dairy products, meat, and dates, which are readily available in the desert.

Bedouin men are known for their traditional dress, which includes a long white shirt, a headscarf, and a cloak called a thobe. They often carry a traditional curved dagger called a khanjar, which is a symbol of their identity and heritage. Bedouin women also have their traditional dress, which includes a colorful dress, a veil, and jewelry.

One of the unique aspects of Bedouin culture in Oman is their hospitality. Bedouins are known for their generosity towards guests and travelers. They often invite strangers into their tents and offer them food, water, and shelter. This tradition of hospitality is deeply ingrained in their culture and is seen as a mark of honor and respect.

Another unique aspect of Bedouin culture in Oman is their love for poetry and storytelling. Bedouins have a rich oral tradition, and they pass down stories and poems from generation to generation. They also have a unique style of poetry called Al Taghrooda, which is a type of improvised poetry that is often recited during social gatherings.

In conclusion, the Bedouin culture in Oman is a unique and integral part of Omani culture. Their traditional lifestyle, customs, and traditions have played a significant role in shaping the country's history and identity. Their hospitality, love for poetry, and storytelling are some of the defining aspects of their culture that continue to thrive in modern-day Oman.

III: Accommodation Tips in Oman

Oman is a beautiful country with plenty of accommodation options to suit all budgets and preferences. Here are some accommodation tips for your trip to Oman:

Hotels: Oman has a wide range of hotels, from luxury 5-star resorts to budget-friendly hotels. Some popular options include the Chedi Muscat, Shangri-La Barr Al Jissah Resort & Spa, and Grand Hyatt Muscat.

Guesthouses: Guesthouses are a great way to experience Omani hospitality and culture. They are usually small and cozy, and you can expect a personal touch from the hosts. Some popular guesthouses in Oman include Al Balid Homestay and The View.

Camping: Camping is a great way to explore Oman's stunning natural beauty. There are plenty of camping sites across the country, including Jebel Shams, Wadi Shab, and Wahiba Sands.

Airbnb: Airbnb is becoming increasingly popular in Oman, and you can find a range of apartments, villas, and houses to rent across the country.

Hostels: Hostels are a great option for budget travelers, and there are a few hostels in Oman that offer affordable accommodation. Some popular options include Mutrah Hotel and Muscat Youth Hostel.

Resorts: Oman has a number of luxurious resorts that offer all-inclusive packages and a range of activities and amenities. Some popular options include Salalah Rotana Resort,

Al Bustan Palace, and Six Senses Zighy Bay.

Regardless of your accommodation preference, be sure to book in advance, especially during peak travel season, to ensure availability and get the best rates.

Affordable Hostels in Oman:list of Hotels

Safeer Plaza Hotel, Al Khuwair, Muscat - Features: Air-conditioned rooms, complimentary breakfast, and Wi-Fi.

Al Falaj Hotel, Muscat - Features: Spacious rooms with balconies, outdoor pool, fitness center, and multiple dining options.

Crystal Suites, Muscat - Features: Modern suites with kitchenettes, complimentary breakfast, and free parking.

Al Murooj Grand Hotel, Salalah - Features: Luxurious rooms with city views, outdoor pool, sauna, and fitness center.

Al Reef Hotel, Seeb, Muscat - Features: Comfortable rooms with air-conditioning, on-site restaurant, and 24-hour front desk.

Majestic Hotel, Muscat - Features: Elegant rooms with flat-screen TVs, rooftop pool, and restaurant with panoramic views.

The Treasure Box Hotel, Muscat - Features: Budget-friendly rooms with modern amenities, on-site restaurant, and free parking.

Safeer Continental Hotel, Muscat - Features: Spacious rooms with work desk, on-site restaurant, and fitness center.

Al Wadi Hotel, Sohar - Features: Comfortable rooms with city views, on-site restaurant, and fitness center.

Pioneer Hotel Apartments, Muscat - Features: Fully furnished apartments with kitchenettes, free Wi-Fi, and on-site laundry facilities.

Please note that prices and availability may vary depending on the season and other factors. It is recommended to check the individual hotel's website or contact them directly for up-to-date information.

IV: Oman Clothing tips According to Seasons

Oman is a country located in the Arabian Peninsula and experiences a hot desert climate, with temperatures remaining high throughout the year. However, there are slight variations in temperature and humidity levels during different seasons. Here are some clothing tips for each season in Oman:

Summer (June to September):

During summer, temperatures can soar up to 50°C (122°F), so lightweight and loose-fitting clothes are essential to stay cool and comfortable. It is recommended to wear light-colored clothing made of breathable fabrics such as cotton, linen, or rayon. Shorts, skirts, and sleeveless tops are suitable for both men and women. Women should carry a scarf or a shawl to cover their heads and shoulders when entering mosques or other religious places.

Autumn (October to November):

Autumn is a transitional season with temperatures ranging from 25°C to 35°C (77°F to 95°F). It is a good idea to wear lightweight long-sleeved tops, pants or jeans, and closed-toe shoes or sandals. A light jacket or sweater may be needed in the evenings, especially in the mountainous regions of Oman.

Winter (December to February):

Winter temperatures in Oman range from 15°C to 25°C (59°F to 77°F). It is advisable to wear warm clothing during the evenings and early mornings. Long pants, long-sleeved tops, and light jackets or sweaters are suitable for this season. Women can carry a shawl or a scarf to cover their heads and shoulders when visiting religious places.

Spring (March to May):

Spring temperatures range from 20°C to 35°C (68°F to 95°F). It is recommended to wear light-colored and breathable clothing made of cotton or linen. Shorts, skirts, and sleeveless tops are suitable for both men and women. A light jacket or sweater may be needed during the evenings, especially in the mountainous regions of Oman.

In summary, when visiting Oman, it is important to choose clothing that is light, loose-fitting, and made of breathable fabrics, regardless of the season. It is also important to respect local customs and wear appropriate clothing when visiting religious places.

V: Omani Food and Drinks.

Oman, a country located on the southeastern coast of the Arabian Peninsula, has a rich culinary tradition that has been shaped by its history and geography. The food in Oman is a reflection of the country's diverse cultural heritage, with influences from Arab, Persian, Indian, and East African cuisine.

One of the most popular dishes in Oman is shuwa, a slow-cooked lamb or goat dish that is marinated in a mixture of spices, then wrapped in banana or palm leaves and roasted in an underground oven. Shuwa is typically served on special occasions, such as weddings and festivals.

Another popular dish in Oman is machboos, a spicy rice dish that is typically made with chicken or fish. The rice is cooked with a blend of spices, including cumin, coriander, turmeric, and cinnamon, and is often served with a side of tomato and onion salad.

Seafood is also a big part of Omani cuisine, with dishes like samak mashwi (grilled fish) and hammour (a type of grouper) being particularly popular. Omani cuisine also features a number of stews and soups, such as harees (a wheat and meat porridge) and shorba (a vegetable soup).

In terms of drinks, coffee is an important part of Omani culture and is often served as a sign of hospitality. Omani coffee is typically served strong and flavored with cardamom. Tea is also popular, with a variety of herbal teas and sweetened milk tea being available.

One unique Omani drink is laban, a salty buttermilk that is often served as a refreshing drink with meals. Other popular non-alcoholic drinks include fresh juices, such as orange and mango, and a sweet, milky drink called sahlab.

For those looking for something stronger, alcohol is available in Oman, but it is only sold in licensed bars and restaurants. Traditional Omani alcohol includes arak, a type of anise-flavored liquor, and sidr honey wine, which is made from the nectar of the sidr tree.

Overall, Omani cuisine offers a rich and diverse array of flavors and dishes that reflect the country's cultural heritage and geography. From slow-cooked meats and spicy rice dishes to refreshing buttermilk drinks and strong coffee, Oman has something to offer for every palate.

VI: Oman Tourist Attractions

Oman is a beautiful country located on the southeastern coast of the Arabian Peninsula. It is known for its stunning natural landscapes, rich cultural heritage, and welcoming people. Here are some of the top tourist attractions in Oman:

Sultan Qaboos Grand Mosque:

This magnificent mosque in the capital city of Muscat is a must-visit attraction for tourists. It features a grand prayer hall, beautiful chandeliers, and a large dome.

Wahiba Sands:

This vast desert offers an amazing landscape of towering sand dunes, making it a popular destination for sand dune bashing, camel riding, and stargazing.

Muttrah Souq:

This traditional market in the city of Muscat offers a wide range of goods, including clothing, jewelry, spices, and souvenirs.

Wadi Shab:

This picturesque wadi is a popular spot for swimming, hiking, and picnicking.

It features crystal-clear pools and waterfalls set against a backdrop of rugged cliffs.

Nizwa Fort:

This 17th-century fort is a testament to Oman's rich cultural heritage. It features a massive circular tower and an impressive collection of artifacts and exhibits.

Jebel Akhdar:

This mountain range offers a cooler climate and stunning views of the surrounding landscape. Visitors can go hiking, rock climbing, or simply enjoy the scenic drives.

Bimmah Sinkhole:

This natural wonder is a limestone crater filled with crystal-clear water. It is a popular spot for swimming and snorkeling.

Salalah:

This coastal city is known for its beautiful beaches, lush greenery, and unique monsoon season, which creates a stunning landscape of waterfalls and greenery.

Al Hoota Cave:

This underground cave system is home to an array of rare and unique animals, including blind fish and bats.

Ras Al Jinz Turtle Reserve:

This protected beach is home to endangered green turtles, which visitors can observe up close during the nesting season.

These are just a few of the many amazing tourist attractions you can visit in Oman. The country offers something for everyone, whether you're interested in history, culture, nature, or adventure.

VII: Car Rental Services/Tour guide companies

There are several car rental companies in Oman that provide rental services to tourists and locals alike. Here are some of the top car rental companies in Oman, along with their addresses:

Europcar Oman - Muscat International Airport, Muscat, Oman

Budget Rent a Car - Muscat International Airport, Muscat, Oman

Avis Oman - Muscat International Airport, Muscat, Oman

Hertz Oman - Muscat International Airport, Muscat, Oman

Sixt Rent a Car - Muscat International Airport, Muscat, Oman

Thrifty Car Rental - Al Khoud, Muscat, Oman

National Car Rental - Al Ghubrah, Muscat, Oman

Dollar Rent a Car - Muscat International Airport, Muscat, Oman

Gulf Car Hire - Way 2559, Al Khuwair, Muscat, Oman

Auto Rent - Al Khuwair, Muscat, Oman

Please note that some car rental companies may have multiple locations throughout Oman, so it's always best to check their website or contact them directly for more information

Oman Tour Guide Companies

There are several tour guide companies operating in Oman that offer a wide range of services for visitors. Here are a few options:

Oman Day Tours: This company provides various day tours and excursions across Oman, including city tours, desert safaris, and dolphin watching trips.

Arabia Horizons Tours: This company offers a range of tours and activities in

Oman, including desert safaris, dhow cruises, and cultural tours.

Muscat Private Tours: This company provides private guided tours of Muscat and other parts of Oman, including historical sites, museums, and natural attractions.

Smart Travel & Tourism: This company offers tailor-made tours and travel packages to various destinations in Oman, including Muscat, Salalah, and Nizwa.

Zighy Tours: This company provides guided tours and outdoor activities, including hiking, camping, and kayaking in Oman's rugged landscape.

These are just a few of the many tour guide companies operating in Oman. Be sure to research and compare different options to find the one that best suits your needs and interests.

VIII: Safety Tips in Oman

Here are some general safety tips to keep in mind when traveling to Oman:

Be aware of your surroundings: Always be aware of what is happening around you, especially in crowded places and tourist areas.

Respect local customs and traditions: Oman is a conservative Muslim country, and it is important to respect local customs and traditions. Dress modestly and behave appropriately in public places.

Carry identification: Always carry your identification with you at all times, as you may be asked to present it by local authorities.

Stay hydrated: Oman can get very hot, especially during the summer months. Drink plenty of water to stay hydrated and avoid heat exhaustion.

Be cautious when driving: Oman has a high rate of road accidents, so it is important to exercise caution when driving. Be sure to follow traffic rules and wear a seatbelt at all times.

Avoid public displays of affection: Public displays of affection are frowned upon in Oman, and could lead to legal trouble.

Don't drink alcohol in public: Alcohol is only allowed in licensed bars and hotels, and it is illegal to drink in public.

Be cautious when swimming: Oman has some beautiful beaches, but it is important to exercise caution when swimming, as currents can be strong and dangerous.

Keep an eye on your belongings: Petty crime, such as pickpocketing and theft, can occur in tourist areas. Keep an eye on your belongings and be cautious of your surroundings.

Know emergency numbers: Be sure to know the emergency numbers in Oman, including the police, ambulance, and fire department.

Printed in Great Britain
by Amazon

26353161R00036